A

Guide

To Modern

Prospecting

Table of Contents

Foreword 4

Chapter 1 6

BUYER PERSONA & ICP 6

Chapter 2 10

EFFECTIVE MESSAGING 10

Chapter 3 16

LEVERAGING TECHNOLOGY & AI 16

Chapter 4 22

Prospecting Strategy 22

Chapter 5 27

TIME MANAGEMENT & WORKFLOW 27

Chapter 6 35

OUTREACH AVENUES & PLATFORMS 35

Chapter 7 42

OBJECTION HANDLING 42

Chapter 8 50

WORKING WITH MARKETING 50

Chapter 9 54

SOCIAL SELLING & CONTENT CREATION 54

Chapter 10	**58**
QUALIFYING QUESTIONS	58
Chapter 11	**66**
MINDSET & ATTITUDE	66
Chapter 12	**72**
MENTORSHIP, CAREER PLANS & GOALS	72
Chapter 13	**76**
SALES ACRONYMS	76
Chapter 14	**79**
STATISTICS	79
Chapter 15	**82**
CAREER GROWTH	82
Professional Experience	**86**
Corey's Biography	**88**
Reference List	**90**

Foreword

In the dynamic landscape of modern sales, the art of prospecting has evolved into a sophisticated and strategic endeavor. As a career coach who has had the privilege of guiding numerous professionals in their journey towards achieving their highest potential, I am thrilled to introduce you to "A Guide to Modern Prospecting" written by my friend, Corey. Corey has masterfully crafted a comprehensive guide that encapsulates his personal experiences and innovative concepts surrounding the initial stages of a sale. This book is not just a compilation of strategies; it is a testament to Corey's profound understanding of what it takes to excel in today's competitive sales environment.

As you delve into this book, you will discover a wealth of knowledge that spans across crucial aspects of prospecting. Corey begins with the fundamentals of defining your Buyer Persona and Ideal Customer Profile (ICP), setting the stage for a targeted approach. He then delves into the nuances of crafting Effective Messaging, emphasizing the importance of personalized communication that resonates with prospects and drives engagement. The inclusion of the "no follow-up or checking in rule" is a testament to Corey's commitment to fostering genuine and meaningful connections.

In a world where technology and AI are revolutionizing industries, Corey offers insightful perspectives on Leveraging Technology + AI, enabling you to harness these tools to streamline your prospecting efforts. His Prospecting Strategy section is a roadmap to success, guiding you through the intricacies of developing a robust and effective plan. Time Management + Workflow is a crucial chapter that addresses the challenges of balancing multiple tasks and maximizing productivity. Corey's practical advice will empower you to optimize your time and work smarter, not harder.

The book further explores Outreach Avenues + Platforms, providing a comprehensive overview of the various channels available for reaching potential clients. Corey's guidance on Overcoming Objections will equip you with the skills to navigate and address concerns with confidence and finesse.

By: Chris Morga, CPCC

Chapter 1

BUYER PERSONA & ICP

Before beginning any sales process or reaching out to prospects, it is crucial to identify and understand your buyer. Thus, whether you are in remote sales, tech sales, SaaS sales, door-to-door, B2B, B2C, medical device sales, car sales, etc. you need a deep understanding of your buyer. So, let's begin with the basics. How do you understand who your buyer is? What is a buyer persona? How do you create a buyer persona or ICP (Ideal Customer Profile)? Why is this so important? There are many ways to understand your buyer and ICP, which we are about to explore.

Before we get ahead of ourselves, let's look at the definitions of an ICP and a buyer persona. According to Adobe Business, a buyer persona is a fictional representation of a key audience segment with a particular interest in your product or business. Also known as a marketing persona, customer persona, or audience persona, buyer personas synthesize all the audience data you collect on your current and ideal customers. A buyer persona uses research to create the ideal customer for you, and also addresses the factors that lead people to the most relevant product for them. Most companies will have more than one buyer persona to effectively target multiple audience segments.

One might wonder, how does a buyer persona differ from an ICP? A buyer persona focuses more on high-level goals based on current customers and other sources, such as industry feedback, by focusing on individual customers within the broader profile to add depth and granularity, while an ICP provides a comprehensive overview of the ideal customer for the entire business. Now that we understand both terms and their differences, let's create our ICP.

Several factors go into creating an ideal customer profile, and a great starting point is reviewing historical data from current and previous customers, regardless of the industry. For example, a medical device company selling surgical equipment will look at the titles they sell to most frequently. If the data shows that 70% of current clients are doctors who perform stomach surgery, this would be critical data for creating an ICP, and thus a great starting point. Additionally, getting feedback from current clients is important. Why? To fully understand their ICP, companies need to identify pain points and know why these specific doctors or companies are buying their product, solution, or software, and what challenges it has helped them overcome. For example, suppose a SaaS (software as a service) company has customers who spend too much time and resources on a particular challenge. In that case, they should define that challenge and understand who the buyer usually is. If 80% of the SaaS company's business comes from selling directly to Chief Marketing Officers, making that title a part of their ICP and primary target for outreach and meetings would be wise. Once your ICP is complete and understood, your chances of success will drastically increase.

In the above example, it would be a wasted effort if a SaaS company employee spent time trying to prospect and sell to the Head of Communications when they only account for 3% of the company's sales. It is also crucial to understand the type of company to pursue. If your company has had major success selling to marketing firms, while having little success selling to communication companies, your focus should be on targeting marketing companies. Before you start your outreach and messaging, ensure that you have considered historical data for both current and previous customers in conjunction with the buyers' titles to kickstart your ICP creation.

There are several important aspects of an ICP that a company should be familiar with. An established ICP enhances sales effectiveness, which leads to better leads, more conversions, and clear focus areas for the sales team. It also aids marketing efforts by allowing for more precise targeting, impacting the cost efficiency by conserving company resources, including money. Additionally, a well-defined ICP helps retain customers as they are more likely to find the value they seek, reducing churn. For the product team, the ICP provides insights into which features to add, improve, or remove. Moreover, an ICP contributes to maintaining a competitive advantage by enabling more personalized targeting based on specific prospect needs. Overall, establishing a meaningful and accurate ICP is critical, not just for the sales department, but for the entire company.

Chapter 2

EFFECTIVE MESSAGING

The importance of effective messaging cannot be overstated and can be approached in a variety of ways depending on the company and/or team. So, what exactly does it mean to have "effective messaging?" It involves creating unique, creative, relevant, and concise messages tailored to the target audience. To boost success and brand awareness, these messages should be delivered through various outreach avenues, such as e-mail, text, LinkedIn, phone, and social selling.

When sending out marketing content, it must be relevant to your target audience and address their challenges. Otherwise, why would anyone open your e-mail, let alone respond to it? The subject line is critical as it is the first thing your audience sees in an e-mail or LinkedIn InMail message, so it needs to be fun, catchy, creative, and unique. Generic subjects like "Just Called You" or "Check This Out!" often lead to no replies or unopened e-mails. Instead, use more appealing subject lines like "Increase Your Revenue with Accurate Healthcare Data" or "Elevate Your Healthcare Data." These specific and tailored subject lines are more likely to result in your e-mails being opened and responded to. Now that we have covered the importance of subject lines, let's discuss the actual content of effective messaging. For example, John works for a SaaS company that sells healthcare software to healthcare companies, targeting their Chief Commercial Officer. An effective message in this scenario would be something like this:

Hi [First Name],

This is John from XYZ Company. We have assisted many similar companies in overcoming healthcare data accuracy challenges, resulting in increased efficiency, cost savings, time savings, and higher sales. Are you available to discuss this next Thursday at 10:00 AM Eastern Time?

Best,

John

Why is this message effective? It is short, simple, and to the point. It begins with a quick introduction to a specific pain point, describes the result of resolving that pain point, and includes a call to action (CTA) with a suggested date and time for a meeting. For those unfamiliar with the term, Investopedia defines a CTA as a marketing term referring to the next step a marketer wants its audience or reader to take. The CTA can have a direct link to sales.

In this example, the CTA is the request to meet at a specific date and time.

Let's also take a glance at what poor messaging looks like.

Hi *(First Name)*,

This is John from XYZ Company. I hope you and your team are doing well and enjoying the beautiful weather today. I'm reaching out because I understand you work in the XYZ department at XYZ Company. Coincidentally, I also work with professionals like you! At XYZ Company, we truly make a difference by supporting companies and teams like yours. One might ask, how? What kind of difference are we making? Great question! Our data is the most accurate on the market, helping teams like yours boost revenue, increase sales, and save time. Additionally, I have attached three PDFs: an overview of our company, a case study of our impact, and the benefits of joining us.

After reviewing the PDFs, please let me know a date and time that works best for you to meet for a 30-minute discussion to see how we can assist you. I look forward to hearing from you and hopefully meeting with you soon.

Regards,

John

If someone sent you that e-mail, would you take the time to read it? Would you open the PDFs and go through them all? Would you respond? I know I wouldn't. This e-mail reeks of desperation, overwhelming the recipient with information overload and a lengthy message that would likely lead the prospect to hit the delete or spam button. Avoid sending an essay filled with redundant words and fluff to your prospect. If I used meaningless sentences and fluff in this book, I could confidently say I would lose the reader's attention, and they would probably close the book and not open it again.

I have found that short, sweet, and simple usually gets the job done. Additionally, the more personalized the e-mail, the higher the chance of getting a reply. However, there is a fine line between spending time creating a personalized e-mail that might bounce back or go to spam and sticking with your original e-mail template. Let's create an example of an effective personalized message. Say you are a sales rep working in SaaS, and your main buyer is the Chief Commercial Officer at a company. From LinkedIn, we learn that this individual's name is Steve. He has been with the company for five years and was recently promoted to his current role of CCO. Steve is also located in Florida, which is the same state as the sales rep. Utilizing this information, a personalized cold e-mail outreach could look something like the following:

Hi Steve,

This is Jim from ABC Company. I noticed you're also in Florida, so I hope you're staying cool in this crazy heat. Congratulations on your recent promotion! I work with many COOs, helping them_____ [insert the problems your solution fixes]. Would it make sense to connect for a brief meeting to learn more about each other's roles and see if we can create any potential synergies?

This is a great example of a concise and personalized e-mail, free from fluff and redundancies. One of my favorite aspects is that we avoided spending 20 minutes stalking their LinkedIn and social media to create a highly tailored e-mail. Over-researching can make the prospect feel "stalked," which can be off-putting. Imagine receiving an e-mail discussing your favorite sports teams, your siblings, where you live, and your dog—you might find it a bit creepy. Instead, we took a quick glance and added just enough personal information without going overboard. I've also seen creative approaches to messaging work well. For instance, a rep creating a brief video on platforms like Vidyard, which requires time and research, can be very effective. This creativity and effort to make a personalized video based on real research increases the chances of the prospect responding and engaging with you. Ask yourself, "If I received this e-mail, would I open it, read it, and reply to it?" If the answer is no, reconsider your approach and strive for more effective messaging. Put yourself in the shoes of the email recipient. Collaborate with your peers, your team, and marketing to brainstorm new strategies to intrigue your target audience, encouraging them to respond, set up meetings, build a pipeline, and close more business, thereby increasing revenue.

Remember, use all avenues of outreach, such as LinkedIn, e-mail, text, and phone calls. The more channels you use, the higher your chances of achieving your desired result. Relying solely on e-mail can result in your messages going directly to spam, with the prospect unaware of your outreach. Using multiple methods increases your chances of making contact. Ultimately, the goal is to get the prospect to engage with you!

Chapter 3

LEVERAGING TECHNOLOGY & AI

Technological advancements and the creation of AI leave companies and their teams asking themselves what software they need and what kind of tech stack is the most efficient and appropriate for their business. AI's formation has become a critical piece of technology in many businesses while also leaving companies wondering how to properly leverage AI. Given the vast array of options available, one could write an entire book on the different choices and the pros and cons of each. So, with all these choices in the marketplace, how do we decide what to use? If you're in a sales role, this decision will likely fall to the leadership team. However, if you work for a smaller company or a startup, and have had significant success in your sales role, your input might be more influential than at a large corporation.

Regardless, knowing what available and which tools to leverage for the best results is crucial, and staying up to date on new technologies is equally as important to stay on pace with your competition. Let's start with choosing a CRM (customer relationship management). This decision depends on various factors, such as the size of the company, the number of users, the budget, the industry, and the company's needs. It wouldn't make sense for a new startup with limited sales to incur a hefty CRM bill. A quick Google search will reveal many CRM options, especially if you are not looking to spend money on solutions like Salesforce or HubSpot, which appear to be the biggest players in the CRM market.

Having experience with both, I personally prefer Salesforce. However, using Salesforce over HubSpot doesn't guarantee a tenfold increase in sales. For me, Salesforce is more user-friendly, better suited to my industry, and helps me keep track of opportunities and activities while staying organized and allowing me to spend less time in my CRM and more time focused on building a pipeline of deals. Nobody wants their manager constantly nagging at them to update their Salesforce or HubSpot deals and opportunities. The rep doesn't want to hear it, and the manager doesn't want to say it, but it still happens, so keep your CRM organized, clean, and up to date.

Selecting a CRM that suits you and your company is critical as prospective employees may turn down job offers solely because they dislike the company's CRM. Many reps live and breathe in their CRM as it is a constant part of their daily workflow. Remember, what works for one company might not work for another. Some CRMs are even designed for specific industries. For instance, life sciences have specialized CRMs, and the same goes for other sectors.

Let's take a quick look at several popular CRMs. According to Forbes, the most popular CRMs, in order, are Zoho, ZenDesk Sell, Monday Sales CRM, Salesforce, and HubSpot. As previously discussed, consider as many variables as possible when selecting your CRM. After picking a CRM, what other technologies and software should be added to a company's tech stack? Obviously, a company needs an e-mail tool. While there are many options, Microsoft Outlook and Gmail seem to be the most popular. Although I prefer Outlook as it integrates seamlessly with most CRMs, Gmail also works well. Choosing an e-mail tool often depends on personal preference and isn't a game-changer in your prospecting efforts.

Next, an effective collaboration and messaging platform is essential. In the 21st century, with the shift to remote work, it's crucial to collaborate with peers to overcome challenges and brainstorm ideas. Easy communication is key in the absence of face-to-face interactions. From my experience, Slack and Microsoft Teams are the most useful platforms. Slack allows easy messaging and quick audio chats with the "huddle" button, while Teams offers similar functionality. Personally, I prefer Slack for peer communication, but Teams may be the best option since most companies use it for meetings. Connecting with prospects via Teams is easier than sending an e-mail with a Zoom link. I tend to avoid Zoom due to its inconvenient chat tool, even though it's a popular option for meetings. Last, but not least, which outreach tool and database should you use? First, ensure that whichever database you choose integrates smoothly with your CRM and outreach tool. I have used many different outreach tools and databases, and my favorite combination to this day is LinkedIn Sales Navigator as a database and Apollo.IO for outreach. I find this combination to be very effective, creating a user-friendly workflow that saves a substantial amount of time prospecting. Many options are available, and the best choice depends on a number of factors as each option has its pros and cons. To name a few databases for prospecting:

- ZoomInfo

- LinkedIn Sales Navigator

- Apollo.io

- Cognism

- RocketReach

- Lusha

Some software options for outreach and sales cadences include:

- SalesLoft

- Yesware

- Apollo.io

- Outreach.io

We have now figured out which CRM, database, and outreach tools to use. So, what's next? Another great addition to your tech stack is software that records meetings and provides a breakdown of key takeaways and challenges discussed using AI. Gong is a fan favorite for this kind of tool as it allows reps to see how others conduct meetings and receive constructive criticism from peers, helping them improve and increase sales. Fathom is a free tool with an AI notetaker so you can sit back and focus on the prospect without needing to focus on taking notes. Having a notetaker on your meetings in my opinion is a game changer. You go from having trouble focusing and listening to the prospect and taking notes to having all your focus on the prospect and don't get distracted to make sure you wrote down a key point.

Leveraging AI in the rapidly changing tech landscape is crucial. AI can be used in many ways, from creating LinkedIn content for your target audience with ChatGPT, to taking notes during meetings, or asking questions and learning. AI should be leveraged! One great use of AI is for inspiration. If you need help creating a LinkedIn post to engage your audience, many AI tools can provide helpful ideas, topics, and content. As an avid LinkedIn user, I find myself utilizing AI nearly every day as I engage with ChatGPT for content inspiration, both for social selling and e-mail generation. If you're not leveraging AI in some form in your day-to-day work, you are likely working inefficiently and falling behind your competitors. Learn how to use AI and make it your ally to work smarter, not harder. The topic of AI can be discussed endlessly, so let's keep it simple: implement some type of AI in your daily work.

Chapter 4
Prospecting Strategy

It goes without saying that a prospecting strategy is of the utmost importance. So, where does one begin to put some paint on the canvas? Now that we have an ICP and a tech stack in place, from a CRM to an outreach tool, this strategy will be easier to create. As mentioned earlier, exploring and utilizing all available outlets for prospecting is essential. Your prospect can quickly do a Google search to learn about you, your role, your company, competitors, and more. With this in mind, developing an effective prospecting strategy in today's world is more challenging than ever due to the vast resources available to prospects.

Let's start with the different ways we can contact prospects. E-mail, text, LinkedIn Connections, LinkedIn InMail's, and cold calling seem to be the most effective. Now, we have the foundation for creating a cadence or sequence with a series of different touchpoints for the prospect. *It might look something like this:*

Day 1 - Touch 1 - E-mail 1 - A/B Test

Day 4 - Touch 2 - LinkedIn Connection

Day 7 - Touch 3 - Message on LinkedIn

Day 8 - Touch 4 - Phone Call

Day 11 - Touch 5 - E-mail 2

Day 14 - Touch 6 - LinkedIn InMail

Day 15 - Touch 7 - Phone Call

Day 16 - Touch 8 - E-mail 3 (final)

Let's break down the above touchpoints to understand what is going on. Once you have found the prospect you want to target, simply add them to your sequence and begin working through the steps. No need to remember which day you left off on, as you can set up your sequence to show tasks on specific days, like day 4, day 7, and day 8. Some outreach platforms can even automatically send e-mails if configured that way in the sequence, which is a feature I utilize while prospecting. For instance, you can have a manual or pre-built e-mail on Day 1 and let the rest run automatically, except for phone calls. With AI, some outreach tools can even leave a voicemail in your voice to a prospect. In the simplest explanation of the touchpoints: on day 1, you will e-mail the prospect; on day 4, you will send a LinkedIn connection; on day 7, you will send a LinkedIn message, and so forth. These e-mails and LinkedIn messages should already be written and built into the appropriate step in the sequence. This way, you are not manually typing up an e-mail for every prospect, which would be very time-consuming.

Instead, you can work smarter with pre-built e-mails. Keeping track of all this is simple, as all your activity will be tracked in your CRM for each specific account/company and the specific prospect within that company. Feel free to create different sequences and test them out to see which one works best. You might be asking, why would I try to contact someone for 16 days with 8 different touchpoints? Great question! This is due to various factors. You don't know if that person is out of the office for a day, took a sick day, or is on vacation. This is why we have multiple touchpoints on different days with gaps in between. Additionally, the 2 to 3-day gaps prevent you from pestering the prospect by sending daily e-mails, which could result in being ignored, blocked, or marked as spam. On a quick side note, avoid prospecting 50 people from the same company simultaneously, as this increases the chances of your e-mails going to spam.

If you feel you must prospect 50 contacts from the same company, it will serve you best to spread it out. You can reach out to 10 on Monday, 10 on Tuesday, 10 on Wednesday, etc., to reduce the chances of your email domain being spam blocked and to keep your email deliverability rate in good standing. If you noticed the mention of "A/B Test" in the first e-mail touchpoint, you might wonder what it is and how to use it. An A/B test helps determine which e-mail gets the most opens and replies, indicating which one works better. For example, if you have 100 prospects, you can split them into two groups: 50 receive E-mail A, and 50 receive E-mail B. Each e-mail has different subject lines and content. If E-mail B gets more opens and replies than E-mail A, you know to stick with E-mail B. This helps you understand what content is effective and where to focus your prospecting efforts moving forward. The point here is that your prospect is not waiting for you to reach out to them. They are likely busy and may check their LinkedIn less frequently than their e-mail, or vice versa. It is imperative to use different outreach channels to reach your prospect because you might not get a response via e-mail or phone, but you may get that response through LinkedIn. For me, without a doubt, LinkedIn is my most effective avenue for prospecting.

For those of you who are analytical and enjoy metrics, I figured I would share some statistics with you. According to Gmass, a marketing and cold e-mail campaign company, the average response rate for a cold e-mail is between 1% and 5%. This means that if you send out 1,000 e-mails, you might only receive 10 to 50 responses. Keep in mind that some of these responses could be negative, such as "Don't contact me again" or "I'm not interested." It's mind-boggling, isn't it? These numbers highlight the need to find ways to stand out from the rest. Despite these low response rates, e-mail remains an excellent avenue for prospecting, booking meetings, building a pipeline, and closing deals. According to Hunter.io, 80% of people prefer that sales reps contact them through e-mail rather than other outlets. So, get your computer and sequences ready, and start sending those e-mails! Keeping these statistics in mind will surely help you build and maintain an effective prospecting strategy and to stay persistent.

Chapter 5

TIME MANAGEMENT & WORKFLOW

Time management is clearly vital and ensuring that your time spent working is effective and yielding results is key. Regardless of the industry or job, time management is a necessary skill to establish, develop, and continue to develop, even if you think you have mastered it. In sales, whether you're an SDR/BDR (sales/business development representative), an Account Executive, in door-to-door sales, B2B, B2C, remote sales, or field sales, managing your time effectively is essential. When done correctly, it can significantly boost your desired outcomes, which in most cases, lead to financial gain.

Exceptional time management skills can help you reach your goals and quotas by allowing you to focus on high-priority, revenue-generating tasks rather than getting bogged down in non-essential work. This skill also helps increase touchpoints, improving your chances of success and better preparation. My personal favorite benefit is stress reduction. Mastering time management reduces stress and worry, leading to a better work-life balance and less feeling of being overwhelmed. This keeps you happier daily, and a happier, less stressed employee will likely achieve greater success (but not true all the time for some). Effective time management in sales also results in a competitive advantage, quicker responses, better resource allocation, strategic planning, and improved professional development through ongoing education and skill enhancement.

For perspective, I don't want you, the reader, to think I am some random person writing a book about prospecting with no proven track record. To share a few credentials, I am regarded as the #1 SDR in company history at two different companies—one private and one publicly traded, and in completely different industries (media and life sciences). I ranked as the #1 SDR month over month and broke every SDR/BDR metric in company history at both companies. These metrics include meetings booked, meetings delivered, qualified opportunities, and, most importantly, revenue to goal. In my last SDR role, I was over 1,300% of my revenue to goal. I have also held three different Account Executive roles strictly focused on new business and all were heavy on prospecting with little to no SDR support. Now that you know I have a track record to back everything up, we can move on. First, we need to establish what effective and reasonable time management looks like. For clarity, let's examine a day in the life of an SDR, Account Executive, or most individual contributor sales roles. A common theme in these roles is how they manage their time. If you're in one of these roles, ask yourself: how, where, and on what is my time spent?

This will give you a foundation to understand where to increase or decrease your time and efforts, ultimately leading to more time spent on revenue-generating activities. Your workflow also ties into your time management skills, which we'll address shortly. If your role mainly involves prospecting, such as an SDR/BDR or some Account Executives who don't have SDR support, here is a time management guide to follow and see how your workflow fits into it.

Let's assume an 8:00 AM start and a 5:00 PM finish. However, I always recommend starting before your peers and finishing after your peers because the more you put in, the more you get out, and my work product is a true testament to that belief as it's a tactic I utilize in my professional role. When you start at 8:00 AM, the first task is to address important, time-sensitive e-mails and LinkedIn messages. After spending about 30 minutes on this, it should be 8:30 AM. Per UpLead, the best times for cold calling are between 10:00 AM and noon as well as late afternoon between 2:00 P.M. and 5:00 PM. This gives us an hour and a half before dialing begins. Try to use this time from 8:30-9:00 AM for breakfast, coffee, a walk, or some stretching if you haven't done so yet. It is now 9:00

AM, with an hour until dialing time. For those in selling roles, this hour can be used for demos, sales presentations, or reviews. If you're an SDR, use this time to research the companies and people you are prospecting. The more you know, the more personalized your approach is, leading to higher engagement from prospects and more meetings booked. li

At 10:00 AM, it's time to start making calls. After a round of calls, it's noon and time for a break. Stretch, have lunch, and get some fresh air. Return to your desk around 12:45-1:00 PM. This period is often when people are out to lunch or taking breaks, so it's not an ideal time for outreach. Instead, use this time to search for prospects on LinkedIn Navigator, ZoomInfo, or Apollo.IO. Once you have your lists, add them to your sequence. However, don't start e-mailing them all at 1:30 PM. Instead, use your outreach tool to schedule e-mails to go out at times when your prospects are likely to be at their desks. Scheduled e-mails are usually best sent in the morning or late afternoon. This scheduling tactic is important for working smarter, not harder. By scheduling e-mails (using pre-built templates in your sequence), you will either wake up to e-mail replies or receive them throughout the day. In my previous role as an SDR, I scheduled hundreds of e-mails, resulting in daily replies showing interest in our services and requesting meetings. My manager often remarked that by 9:00 AM, I had already sent over 100 e-mails, which fascinated the entire company. I wasn't doing anything that required me to be a rocket scientist, I was just working in a smart, effective manner. This high level of activity and productivity was significantly aided by the scheduling of e-mails, which will surely get your managers' attention in a positive way.

The time is now 2:30 PM. You've already answered e-mails, made phone calls, prospected, researched, and scheduled e-mails while taking breaks as needed. Quite a productive day, and it's only 2:30, likely placing you ahead of your peers on a productivity scale. Now is a good time to send out some e-mails and complete tasks in your sales cadence as most people are back from lunch. At 3:00 PM, it's time to smile and dial! Hit the phones hard for an hour with full focus, confidence, and no distractions. If needed, block off your calendar every day from 3:00 to 4:00 PM. When 4:00 P.M. comes, take a 10–15-minute breather after that power hour of dialing. You earned it! The last 45 minutes of your day should include a bit of everything: answer e-mails that came in during the day, make call-backs to prospects, add prospects to your cadence, and schedule e-mails. At 5:00 PM, it's time to call it a day! Talk about a productive day. Imagine using this formula every day—rinse and repeat. This is how time management, workflow, and structuring your day should look if your role is heavy on prospecting and booking meetings, and even for sellers/individual contributors who don't do enough presentations or demonstrations and need to fill their calendar. See below for a simple time management guide without all the explanations and reasoning.

8:00 - 8:30 AM - Reply to e-mails

8:30 - 9:00 AM - Coffee, food, stretch, walk, clear your head for the day.

9:00 - 10:00 AM - Demos, Sales Presentations, and researching.

10:00 - 12:00 PM - Smile and Dial

12:00 - 12:45/1:00 PM - Lunch, walk, personal calls, etc.

1:00 - 2:30 PM - Add prospects/contacts to the sales sequence and schedule e-mails

2:30 - 3:00 PM - Complete tasks due in the sales sequence

3:00 - 4:00 PM - Smile and Dial

4:00 - 5:00 PM – 10 to 15-minute breather, answer e-mails, and schedule e-mails.

One additional point I want to make before moving on, which I am sure may be met with disagreement from some sales leaders, sales managers, SDRs, AEs, or any individual contributor, is about VOLUME. I practice what I preach. Many people emphasize quality over quantity and personalizing your touches. While personalized touches can engage your prospect, imagine spending 15 minutes "stalking" someone's LinkedIn and other platforms to create a highly personalized e-mail, only for it to go to spam, bounce, or hit a firewall. It's not an ideal use of time if you ask me and can lead to a lot of wasted time and frustration.

Here's the logic behind advocating for a mass volume of outreach. Consider this analogy: A man named Jim goes on dates with 100 different women over the course of a year, while another man, Joe, goes on dates with just 5 women in the same period. Both want the same result—to get into a serious relationship. Who do you think has a better chance of achieving the desired results? I would bet on Jim, and if Vegas could create odds on this, I have no doubt that Jim would be the favorite by a long shot. Here is another analogy to consider: if Ken and Josh go fishing and Ken puts out 100 fishing lines and Josh puts out only 10 fishing lines, who do you think has a better chance of catching a fish or the most fish? If I was a betting man, my money would be on Ken to get the first fish and the most fish.

Personally, I have always believed in firing off as many emails and messages as possible. By combining massive outreach volume with quality messaging, the more likely you are to hit your requisite numbers. I live and die by this volume tactic and have a proven record to demonstrate its success. Although there are some people out there who may disagree with me, and that is fine, I rely on what has proven successful for me, and you should do the same. To this day, I still send out at least 200 emails a day, but, having said that, I use Apollo.IO's automatic feature to assist me. This is a prime example of working smarter, not harder, and putting the above techniques to use. You may be asking, "well, don't you get spam blocked?" or "are all these emails getting through to the recipient?" A personal strategy I use to prevent my e-mails from being spam blocked or ruining the company domain goes something like this: let's say you have 100 contacts that work at XYZ company that you would like to prospect. I would enroll each of them into a sequence, but rather than e-mailing all in one day, I would send 10 per day (10 on Monday, 10 on Tuesday, 10 on Wednesday, and so on until you hit the 100). This strategy has proven effective in prospecting a large number of potential clients, so I would highly recommend that you implement it in your prospecting routines.

Chapter 6

OUTREACH AVENUES & PLATFORMS

We have briefly touched on different outreach avenues and platforms, but not in depth. Let's dive straight in. What exactly is considered an outreach avenue or platform? In my own words, it is any method through which you can potentially contact a prospect. Many different outreach avenues and platforms exist, especially thanks to recent technological advancements. When contacting prospects, it is essential to use multiple avenues; thus, even if you have the most success with e-mail, it's imperative that you do not abandon other avenues. Here's an analogy to explain my reasoning: if you had a million dollars to invest in the stock market, would it be wise to put the entire amount into one stock?

I'm not a financial advisor, but I bet 99% of financial advisors would say that's an awful idea. The financial advisor would most likely recommend spreading the money out into different investments, enhancing diversity. You don't want to put all your eggs in one basket, right? The same theory applies to prospecting. My personal favorite platform to engage with prospects and book meetings is LinkedIn. LinkedIn is a huge part of my "secret sauce." When you connect with someone, they can see your picture, location, job, company, experience, content, and more. This already adds a bit of personalization to your outreach without even trying. If you're sending an e-mail, the recipient has no idea who you are, where you're from, or what you do. The chances that someone you are prospecting via e-mail will look you up on LinkedIn are slim. My best practice is to send a LinkedIn connection request to a prospect without a note or message, and once they accept, that's when I send them a message. Pro tip: don't expect to just send one LinkedIn message to a prospect to book a meeting. From personal experience, the likelihood of booking a meeting following the first LinkedIn message is between 1% to 5%.

Thus, I highly recommend staying persistent by sending the prospect one message a week until you receive a reply. Yes, some people will find it annoying, but honestly, who cares. You're in sales and if you can't handle rejection, you are in the wrong field. Remember, prospects aren't sitting at their computer on LinkedIn waiting for your message. What's the worst possible scenario here if you keep following up? Maybe they would contact your manager and say how "annoying" you are. I've seen this happen before and the manager usually praises the salesperson for their persistence and relentlessness. Moreover, as you build connections in your industry, you'll have more "mutual friends," similar to Facebook, thus increasing your chances of an accepted connection request. LinkedIn sets a weekly limit of 100 connection requests per user, which resets every Monday. I highly recommend maxing out this limit each week. Keep in mind that you can see when someone reads your message on LinkedIn. Use that to your advantage. When following up if you see that the prospect hasn't read your message maybe wait another week to see if they read it or not. If it's been two weeks and they haven't read it then feel free to send them a message. It's very possible your message is at the bottom of their inbox and a new message will bring it back to the surface. LinkedIn is my absolute favorite platform for engagement, networking, prospecting, and research. I cannot recommend it enough.

Additionally, when using LinkedIn Sales Navigator, you should be getting 50 free InMail credits a month. An InMail on LinkedIn is a direct message to your prospect's inbox with a subject line. Regardless of whether you are connected, they will receive the message. These credits accumulate over time, so if you don't use your 50 credits in one month, they carry over into the next month. I would say about 90-95% of the demos I had via LinkedIn are from a second or third message after a connection and not via InMail. However, InMail can still result in responses from prospects and it's a great tool to use if your prospect won't accept your invite, but you are still trying to get in touch. Additionally, 75-80% of the demos I have had in general are from LinkedIn. Use it to your advantage!

The good old-fashioned cold calling still works! Believe it or not, this is another method you can, and should, incorporate into your prospecting efforts. Cold calling seems daunting for reps in their 20s and 30s because it's considered "old-fashioned," but it works! I was actually able to source the largest deal of my sales career from a cold call. There's no need to be shy or afraid to pick up the phone. If you make a mistake or say something incorrect, that's completely fine. That's how we learn and grow. At the end of the day, what's the worst thing that could happen? Someone might say no or tell you to go away, and then you move on to the next prospect. Even if they curse you out, it's not a big deal. Don't take it personally, you're just doing your job.

Regarding the phone, you can also utilize texting/SMS with the database and outreach tools we discussed earlier. If you only have a prospect's mobile number and can't get through, shoot them a text. Keep it simple and short, like:

"Hi John, Jim here with ABC Company. We help companies like yours streamline and automate marketing efforts to generate leads, leading to a 200% increase in sales for our clients. Worth a chat?"

It's best to keep it short, sweet, and simple while including a quick intro, your pitch, and the results of your solution. Nobody wants to read an essay on any platform. Especially when dealing with C-Suite executives, get to the point and keep it brief.

E-mail is a given, but for those who don't know, you must also e-mail your prospects as part of your outreach efforts. This helps familiarize your prospects with you, your company, your solution, and your brand, even if they never respond. With e-mail, you can attach relevant screenshots, including video links, case studies, a solution PDF overview, a personalized video, and more. You might send 10 different e-mails to the same person over the course of a month with no replies. This is why you need to utilize multiple outreach avenues. I have often been ignored by e-mail, but I connected and set up a meeting via LinkedIn with the same prospect. In addition, I have been ignored on LinkedIn but got a response via e-mail, a cold call, or even a text.

There are proper and improper ways to utilize e-mail effectively. Sending long e-mails is not effective. However, short, simple e-mails that get to the point are more effective. Depending on the outreach tool you use, you should be able to see who opened your e-mail and how many times. The same applies to those who clicked a link, or a PDF attached to your email. Being able to track those engaging with your e-mails is a good indicator of interest, which should motivate you to capitalize on the potential opportunity. In that case, if the prospect fails to respond, I would pick up the phone and call. Utilize the analytics and outreach tools you have to help improve your outreach, increase your lead generation, and book more meetings.

We have established several outreach avenues and essential platforms for prospecting efforts, including LinkedIn, cold calling, text/SMS, and e-mail. So, what other avenues are available to connect with prospects and generate interest or engagement? Social media is another outlet to reach prospects, but it can be tricky. For example, when using Instagram, Facebook, X, or TikTok, prospects will see your personal, not professional, profile. Depending on your content, this can either be beneficial or detrimental. Prospects might question how you found their profiles or even feel uncomfortable, potentially pushing them away. Social media for prospecting is a slippery slope that I avoid, though some people find success with it. Suppose you choose to use social media for prospecting. In that case, I recommend targeting only those individuals you have previously messaged or e-mailed but couldn't secure a meeting with.

This approach is more familiar and less likely to come across as "stalking." Prospecting via social media platforms is personally my least favorite way to prospect, and although I don't get many results from it, that doesn't mean someone else can't. Referrals are critical and can be an easy and effective way to target specific prospects. If a client is happy with your product, ask if they know anyone who might be interested and request an introduction. Be included in the e-mail thread so you can introduce yourself directly. Additionally, if your company has a department or employee dedicated to strategic partnerships or alliances, connect with them to see how they can help you get your foot in the door with specific accounts or prospects.

In conclusion, it is of the utmost importance to use various outreach avenues. While focusing on the avenue that brings you the most success, do not abandon other methods. Continue to work on all of them for the best results. Remember, stay persistent, stay relentless, and do not stop until you get a reply from the prospect.

Chapter 7

OBJECTION HANDLING

No matter what field you are in, even if it's not sales, you will encounter objections at some point in your career and day-to-day work. You may also face many of these objections in your personal life. How you handle objections can determine whether you get a meeting with a prospect, gain engagement and interest, close a deal or have the prospect walk away and go with a competitor. Objections are usually specific to the conversation and the product, software, solution, medical device, etc., you are selling.

Remember, the key point of sales is not that you are in the business of sales but that you are in the business of problem-solving. Your product, software, etc., should solve their problems. Don't start listing out all the features and benefits for no reason. Understand your prospects' needs and explain how your solution can fix their needs. A great salesperson often helps prospects realize problems and challenges before they are even aware of them. If a prospect doesn't understand how you can help solve their problem with the desired results, your chances of closing a deal are slim, even if you handle objections well. What are the most common objections, and how does one handle them effectively?

Let's begin with cold calling. The most common objections are:

- *"I am too busy to talk right now."*

- *"I'm not interested."*

- *"I'm in a meeting." (This always makes me laugh because who would pick up the phone from an unknown number during a meeting?)*

- *"Send me some info."*

- *"Is this a sales call?"*

Looking at these objections individually, let's start with "I am too busy to talk right now." If someone picks up your phone call, they likely aren't too busy to talk; otherwise, why would they have picked up? They probably just think you are an annoying salesperson or that it's a scam. Quickly respond with, "No problem, I am busy also so this will only take a minute. Does that work for you?" You will either get hung up on or get a "Yes, I have a minute." By saying to the prospect that you are also busy is elevating your status in the prospects mind. Meaning even if it's your first job and cold call ever you don't want them to think that. You would want them to think you are a successful, a busy person, and you found the time to make a quick phone call. Fake it till you make it! Handling objections, no matter how good you are, doesn't mean you will succeed 100% of the time. If you call enough people, you will get hung up on at some point, no matter how good you are. It's just a fact of sales and cold calling.

The objection "I'm not interested" often follows a 30-second elevator pitch. Instead of a quick pitch, try instilling curiosity and pinpointing specific problems the prospect might have to engage back. This strategy helps avoid objections altogether. However, if you encounter it, respond with questions like, "How are you handling this today?" or "Is your current solution achieving the desired results?" These questions will likely trigger curiosity and engagement rather than shutting down the conversation. The "I'm in a meeting" excuse is my absolute favorite, and it amuses me whenever I hear it. If you were in a meeting and saw an unknown number, would you pick up the phone? Probably not! I know I wouldn't. My go-to response for this comical objection is, "No problem, I have a meeting in two minutes, so this will be brief." This reassures the prospect that the call will be short and increases the chances they will stay on the phone. Additionally, it subtly suggests that you are also busy and important, which can elevate your status in their mind as we just went over.

"Send me some info" might be the most annoying objection because it leaves you in limbo without a clear yes or no. You're not exactly sure if they are saying this because they actually want more information or if it's just a softer way of being told to screw off. If you hear this, it likely means you didn't trigger enough curiosity or pain points during the call. To address it, you can say, "Sure, but while I have you..." and try to re-engage with curiosity and pain points. Alternatively, you can ask, "Sure, what is your best e-mail?" This allows you to get their contact information, send the requested info, and continue following up, potentially with another call if they don't respond to your e-mail. With the email outreach tool, you will also be able to track if they open and click links in your email, thus letting you know if they wanted the info or were just saying it to get you off the phone.

"Is this a sales call?" is a common objection that most people encounter when making cold calls. A simple and effective response to this objection can be, "No, I'm calling to see if we can help you solve [problem], leading to [desired result]." After all, we are in the business of problem-solving. Another response could be, "Technically, yes, but I'm not in sales; I'm in the business of solving my clients' problems." This response will immediately trigger curiosity and likely engage the prospect. Your prospect will not be used to hearing that reply and it comes with a certain degree of confidence. Now that we have covered some common objections in cold calls, let's move on to objections during sales presentations, demos, field sales conversations, door to door sales etc. The most common objections reps face in these situations are:

- *"It is too expensive."*

- *"I have never heard of your company."*

- *"I don't see how this can help solve [problem]."*

- *"The timing isn't right."*

- *"Why would I go with you instead of [competitor]?"*

Let's tackle these objections individually, starting with the first: "It's too expensive." Keep in mind that spending money involves financial risk, and nobody wants to make a large purchase without good reason. Additionally, you might not be effectively displaying the value your offering brings. A great response could be, "What would it cost you and your company if you didn't solve [problem]?" This response engages the prospect and makes them focus on their pain points and challenges. While cost matters, remember that you are giving a sales presentation, a demo, or having an in-person discussion, so the prospect must have some level of interest and be aware of the challenges they need help with. In addition, in many cases, one's solution can also lead to cost savings which can certainly help bring your prospects guard down in making a financial decision. A powerful tool to handle financial objections is an ROI calculator, so if your company has one, capitalize on it as it will allow the prospect to see the financial gains of implementation, bringing you closer to a deal.

"I have never heard of your company" is a common objection, depending on where you work. If you work for a mega-corporation like Amazon or Google, you won't hear this much, but in most cases, you will. Prospects often have a hard time buying from a company they are unfamiliar with, usually due to a lack of trust and credibility. Ensure you elevate your status in the prospect's mind and build rapport and credibility during your presentations to avoid this objection. If you encounter this objection, a great response is, "I don't hear that often, but we work with many companies similar to yours, such as ABC Company and DEF Company, helping them with XYZ." This effective response builds industry credibility and trust while addressing their pain points. Moreover, if you get this objection, feel free to volunteer a list of current clients that the prospect may be familiar with.

"I don't see how this can help solve XYZ" is an objection you really want to avoid. If you receive this objection, it likely means you have done a poor job explaining your solution and how it can fix the XYZ problem. It's also possible you did a poor job in your discovery when you were trying to uncover specific pain points and tying those pain points to your solution. Regardless, you need to respond effectively. Your best bet is to ask a question, such as, "Is there something specific you would like me to dive deeper into or elaborate on?" Alternatively, you could ask, "Is there something you would like to review to gain clarity?" Your tone will also play a role when asking this as you want to sound curious and not upset or frustrated. If you prefer not to ask a question, consider how you can avoid this objection all together or how to better explain your solution to address the prospect's pain points and clearly illustrate how it can solve XYZ.

"The timing isn't right" objection always gets under my skin. Why? It means they understand your solution and have some interest, but they aren't fully convinced you can solve XYZ for them. It also leaves the rep unsure whether this is an honest objection or a polite brush-off. If you are triggering curiosity, elevating your status as an industry expert, and solving problems effectively, this objection shouldn't arise. However, if you do encounter it, use it as an opportunity to ask questions and gain further clarity. Ask, "Can you elaborate on what you mean when you say the timing isn't right?" Another effective question is, "I completely understand. Could you tell me when you think the timing would be right?" Another good reply could be "Ah I see, I am assuming you just either renewed or switched vendors" this way you may at least gather some important intel. If these questions aren't effective and the prospect remains unresponsive, agree with them and say, "No problem at all. When does the timing work better for you? I will send you a placeholder meeting invite a few weeks before." This keeps the deal alive and helps determine if the prospect is genuine or if it's just the wrong time due to factors like company layoffs, budget cuts, new leadership, or restructuring. "Why would I go with you instead of XYZ?" is a common objection. As mentioned earlier, you receive most of these objections because you haven't effectively highlighted the prospect's current pain points and how your solution addresses them. So, how should you handle this objection? Many teams use a one-page comparison sheet that outlines what each company offers. You can share this with the prospect, explain it, and emphasize how your solution more effectively addresses their issues. It's also important to avoid bad-mouthing/reviling competitors.

Another response, depending on your confidence level, could be, "You are more than welcome to shop around with our competitors and reach back out to me." In my experience, focusing on the desired outcome and results rather than just making the sale increases your chances of success. This approach to handling objections can feel risky but is often very effective. If you're not confident or comfortable with these methods, go back to basics. Focus on the question and provide a clear, appropriate answer explaining why they should choose your solution over the competitor's.

Chapter 8
WORKING WITH MARKETING

Marketing is a crucial department in every company as it plays a vital role in supporting sales teams and prospecting efforts, including both inbound and outbound leads. It also focuses on brand awareness, credibility, educating prospects and the market, sales collateral, market research, messaging, and running campaigns. Let's explore each of these areas to understand the roles marketing and sales play and how they interconnect.

Marketing generates leads for the sales team through campaigns designed to attract potential customers. These leads, known as MQLs (marketing-qualified leads), are distinguished from SQLs (sales-qualified leads). MQLs are based on specific criteria and fit, while SQLs are MQLs that have been further evaluated by the sales team. SQLs generally show more engagement than MQLs. MQLs are valuable because they enhance sales team efficiency, increase lead conversions, and allow for personalized and targeted strategies. In some cases, MQLs are prospects further along in the buying process. Marketing also plays a key role in brand awareness, significantly impacting the sales team and the company. Brand awareness involves creating content, such as videos, blogs, and articles, that the sales team can utilize. Social media is another marketing tactic to engage audiences, collaborate with influencers, and post consistently, often generating MQLs for the sales team. Advertising, including commercials, digital ads, and traditional methods, contributes to brand awareness. Additionally, marketing efforts in SEO, PR, e-mail marketing, co-branding, cross-promotions, product demos, referral programs, and community events are essential for creating brand awareness, leading to positive results and leads for both the marketing and sales teams.

Credibility is crucial in any industry for companies and individuals alike. This raises the question: how does one establish credibility for a company, a product, or themselves? A key component is producing high-quality content and educational resources, such as webinars, eBooks, and whitepapers. When potential prospects download an eBook or attend a webinar, they are added to a list from which leads are generated. Credibility is also built by managing reviews on platforms like Yelp and Google and creating success stories from current or previous customers. Consistent branding, industry awards, certifications, networking, ethical business practices, and relationship-building further enhance credibility. If your marketing team has established credibility in your market, you have a significant advantage in gaining access to companies or individuals. Credibility developed by marketing over time can significantly impact the success or failure of a sales team. Similarly, educating prospects and the market is vital for marketing and sales. Marketing teams use various tactics to educate the market and buyers, such as blogs, articles, whitepapers, and eBooks. Educated buyers facilitate a smoother sales process for the sales team. Other educational tactics include online workshops, webinars, newsletters, explainer videos, real-world evidence examples, and interactive content, all of which enable the sales team.

Market research is integral to a marketing team's daily activities, ultimately benefiting the sales team. Marketing gathers and analyzes various data types through surveys, software, quantitative and qualitative analysis, observations, interviews, focus groups, and questionnaires. This data helps determine where marketing and sales should focus their efforts. One of the most valuable contributions of marketing is the creation of sales collateral, equipping the sales team with resources for prospecting and the sales cycle. Sales collateral includes PDFs of specific use cases, real-world evidence, success stories, video links, and educational resources. It is crucial that marketing creates high-quality and effective sales collateral, and that the sales team leverages these resources. In some cases, the marketing team creates messaging for the sales team and runs campaigns to generate leads, which flow to the sales team. They use market research, data, interviews, and success stories to craft effective messaging. The types of campaigns they create include brand awareness, lead generation, product launches, sales promotions, customer retention, events, content, and social media. These campaigns ultimately lead to positive results for the company and the sales team. It is essential for marketing and sales to work in harmony to achieve success.

From my personal experience, working with marketing can be very beneficial. Although I didn't rely on the marketing department at the beginning of my career, I wish I had as I've been able to recognize the number of benefits provided through collaboration. My favorite benefit has been receiving specific documents and/or resources to send to prospects. I have found that if you can provide visuals while prospecting, it helps the prospect's understanding and engagement. To provide the prospect with visuals, I have utilized both the generic PDFs created by the marketing department and have asked the team to create a tailored PDF based on the prospects interest. Furthermore, the marketing team may be able to advise you what techniques have proven successful for them and those not as successful, allowing you to piggyback off the success for sales engagement. All in all, I highly encourage setting up internal meetings with your marketing department to bounce ideas off one another and see where it takes you because the chances of you walking away with something beneficial are high.

Chapter 9

SOCIAL SELLING & CONTENT CREATION

According to Sprout Social, social selling is a lead-generation strategy that helps salespeople interact directly with prospects through social platforms. This concept challenges the typical transaction experience between customers and companies, fostering more natural relationships with leads. Social selling is essential for generating leads, making it a crucial strategy for sales professionals. So, how does one engage in social selling and utilize it to their benefit? Social selling generally involves some form of content creation. The different types of social selling include LinkedIn, X, Facebook, content-based, engagement-based, influencer-based, and event-based social selling.

As I mentioned earlier, LinkedIn selling is my favorite form of social selling because I have found the best results with that platform. However, everyone should use the type of social selling that yields the best results for them. First, ensure your LinkedIn profile is optimized correctly. It must look professional and attractive to encourage prospects to view your profile and engage with your posts. Use InMail's, posts, groups, and polls on LinkedIn to gain interest, attract prospects, and generate leads. Content creation is crucial; post relevant, educational, and engaging content to attract your desired audience.

Platforms like X and Facebook are more social media driven but do require content creation. Replying to tweets, sharing relatable content, and monitoring trends and specific conversations on X are a few ways to utilize it for social selling. The same applies to Facebook, but the strategy is slightly different. Start by creating a business page or group and sharing unique content to establish a solid foundation for your Facebook social selling efforts.

Engagement-based social selling differs from social selling via X, Facebook, and LinkedIn because it requires monitoring tools, such as Sprout Social, Hootsuite, or Brandwatch, to track specific hashtags or keywords related to your industry. This helps you stay current on important news and information, identify where to prospect, and create engagement. Engagement-based social selling can also be done through online communities, such as forums or industry groups. Influencer-based social selling is fun but may require some capital. Collaborating with an influencer on Instagram to put out content geared toward your solution can be costly, depending on their follower count. Ensure the influencer has a voice in your industry to avoid wasting money. You can create partnerships with influencers to co-host events or content, promoting your brand, products, or solution. Utilizing an influencer's network can help you reach a broader market and even participate in event-based social selling, including hosting webinars, conferences (in-person or virtual), X chats, industry topics on X, and going live on Facebook and Instagram.

The content used in these social selling tactics is crucial to their success. Key elements of effective content include high quality, educational value, interactive calls to action, visual appeal, originality, accuracy, honesty, relevance, value, and personalization. Mastering these content creation keys sets you up for success in social selling.

Here are some keys and tips for success in content creation:

1. **Set Goals and Define Objectives:** Establish clear KPIs (key performance indicators) to have measurable data and track the success of your content.
2. **Use Analytics Tools:** Maintain the measurement of your content's success with the help of an analytics tool.
3. **Know Your Audience:** Understanding your audience, similar to defining your ICP (ideal customer profile), is crucial. Conduct research on your prospects and tailor specific content to your targeted audience.

4. **Create High-Quality Content:** Stand out by producing creative and high-quality content. Ensure that your content always brings value.
5. **Fact-Check:** Maintain your credibility by fact-checking your content to avoid errors.
6. **Stay Updated on Trends:** Keep up with important industry trends and incorporate them into your content creation.

Following these keys and tips should help you achieve greater success and desired results in your content creation efforts.

Chapter 10
QUALIFYING QUESTIONS

Qualifying questions are an essential part of prospecting and the sales process. They help both parties save time by determining early on if there is a mutual fit and if the prospect is a qualified buyer. These questions are typically tailored to the specific product, software, medical device, or service being sold.

Some companies use a qualification method called BANT, but what does BANT even mean?

- ➢ Budget
- ➢ Authority
- ➢ Need
- ➢ Timeline

Understanding these elements is crucial throughout the sales process, especially during prospecting. For instance, if during one's prospecting efforts, it is revealed that the prospect has a budget allocated for the solution, has the authority to make a purchase, needs the solution, and has an immediate or short timeline, that is what I like to refer to as a homerun. However, getting a prospect to disclose this information during a cold call is usually challenging.

Prospects are typically reluctant to share such details with someone they don't know or haven't researched. Navigating BANT during a cold call or e-mail is tricky but obtaining information on even one or two of these fields can provide a significant advantage in qualifying the prospect and creating an effective sales plan.

Effective qualifying questions can be categorized into areas, such as needs and challenges, budget, decision-making power, timeline, fit and suitability, existing solutions and competition, pain points, strategic alignment, and logistics and implementation. Some of these categories are best addressed throughout the sales process rather than during initial cold outreach. Nonetheless, being familiar with all types of qualifying questions is important.

The following is a list of some of the most important qualifying questions to ask:

Needs and Challenges

- ➢ What are the biggest challenges you're currently facing in your business?
- ➢ What are your top priorities for the next quarter/year?
- ➢ What solutions have you tried in the past to address these challenges?

Budget

- What budget have you allocated for this project/solution?
- How do you prioritize spending in this area?
- Are you currently using any solutions that you're paying for?

Authority and Decision-Making

- Who is involved in the decision-making process for this type of purchase?
- What is your role in the decision-making process?
- How does your company typically make decisions on new purchases?

Timeline

- What is your timeline for implementing a solution?
- Are there any specific deadlines or timeframes you need to meet?
- When are you looking to make a decision?

Fit and Suitability

- What features or capabilities are most important to you when creating a solution?
- How do you envision our product/service fitting into your current operations?
- What would a successful outcome look like for you?

Existing Solutions and Competition

- Are you currently using a similar product/service? If so, what do you like or dislike about it?
- What prompted you to look for a new solution now?
- Have you evaluated any other solutions? What stood out to you about them?

Pain Points and Motivations

- What happens if you don't address this issue now?
- How would solving this problem impact your business?

Strategic Alignment

- How does this initiative align with your company's strategic goals?
- What internal or external factors are driving this need?

Logistics and Implementation

- What kind of support or training would you need for implementation?
- How will you measure the success of this solution?

Now that we have established qualifying questions, it's clear that you can't ask all of them during a cold call or most types of cold outreach. If you try to keep the prospect on the phone to answer 20 questions, they will likely hang up or tell you to leave them alone since they don't know you and no rapport or credibility has been built yet. This brings us to a critical point: determining the best qualifying questions to ask during cold outreach to avoid scaring off the prospect.

Some of my favorite questions to ask during cold outreach are:

"Are you familiar with XYZ company or with XYZ solution?"

"How are you currently addressing XYZ problem?"

"Are you currently using something (software, CRM, med device, solar panels, etc.) to solve for XYZ?"

"Is this solution that solves for XYZ an item to which the budget has been allocated?"

I tend to avoid asking questions like "Are you the decision maker?" because these types of questions can come off as rude and too straightforward. Additionally, it's 2024, and with technology platforms like LinkedIn, Google, and ZoomInfo, you usually already know the prospect's title, giving you a strong indication of their influence in the decision-making process. For example, if you are selling software that solves problems for sales teams, you will know that an entry-level sales rep has significantly less decision-making power compared to that of the head of sales.

An example of a simple and effective cold call with qualifying questions might look something like this:

Rep: Hi John, this is Jim with XYZ Company, calling regarding the CRM your company uses.

Prospect: Hi, do I know you?

Rep: We connected on LinkedIn recently, and I noticed you might be experiencing similar difficulties to what I've heard from others in the industry.

Prospect: What difficulties are you referring to?

Rep: Good question. How are you currently addressing the time your reps waste inputting notes into your CRM and logging everything correctly when they could be spending more time selling?

Prospect: Ummm... well... I haven't really thought about that. But now that you bring it up, it's something to consider.

Rep: Sure thing! What CRM are you using now, and do you have a budget allocated for additional solutions?

Prospect: We're using Salesforce and have some extra funds, but I don't make these decisions. However, I may have some influence.

Rep: Fair enough. We've helped many similar companies using Salesforce. What date and time next week works best for a brief meeting to learn more about each other and see if we might be a good fit for your company?

Prospect: How about 10:00 AM EST on Thursday?

Rep: Perfect, that works. What's your best work e-mail for the calendar invite?

Prospect: John@xyz.com

Rep: Great. I just e-mailed you the calendar invite and look forward to speaking with you then, on Thursday.

This example nicely illustrates how the rep asks qualifying questions, encouraging the prospect to reveal important information without feeling intimidated or wasting their time. Although not all aspects of BANT were covered, the rep gains a basic understanding of the prospect's situation and can delve into more details and qualifying questions during the initial meeting. This example also demonstrates how to keep a call short and to the point, avoiding wasted time for both parties. Additionally, it shows how to quickly build rapport with a simple mention like "We connected on LinkedIn recently." However, only say this if it's true — lying to a prospect will usually come back to haunt you. From my own experience as an SDR, I was repeatedly advised to get BANT information before the initial meeting. Because gathering all the BANT information is very difficult to do, especially on the first cold interaction, I would gather the most information I could without asking too much or risking losing the meeting because I knew the AE would seek out all necessary information during the demo or presentation.

To get as much BANT information as I could without imposing too much, I would ask the basic questions, such as "are you familiar with XYZ software" or "how are you handling (insert pain point) today"? Questions like these got the prospect talking, which usually allowed me to gather BANT information without directly asking Additionally, thanks to technology, and specifically LinkedIn, you will most likely know before reaching out if the prospect has some decision-making power based on his/her title. Thus, you likely have your "A" in BANT before you even reach out. Strategically speaking, I always tried to get at least one letter of BANT during my initial outreach because that meant I really had two, assuming I knew the prospect's title beforehand.

Chapter 11
MINDSET & ATTITUDE

Mindset and attitude are crucial for achieving anything you set your mind to. I have even seen people get fired, not for poor work, but for having a poor attitude that seeped into their peers' attitudes. A poor mindset usually leads to poor results, while a positive mindset tends to yield positive outcomes. In sales, maintaining a positive mindset is essential for a lasting career, preventing burnout, and achieving or exceeding your goals. Being a sales rep requires a special kind of person, and it's not for everyone. Then again, that could be said about most careers. If you believe you have what it takes to succeed in sales, go for it. Your day-to-day attitude significantly influences your success or failure. You should also surround yourself with the type of people you want to eventually become like. If you surround yourself around a bunch of sales reps who hate their jobs and are always complaining, chances are you may become that one day. If you wake up thinking, "Ugh, I don't want to do this today. I hate this. Even if someone picks up, they'll just hang up on me," your chances for success aren't great. However, if you wake up thinking, "Today I have to make 100 phone calls, and I am sure I'll book some meetings," you'll likely see more positive results.

Creating a positive and resilient mindset is another key to success. Positive thinking often leads to positive results. Have you ever read the book The Secret? If not, I encourage you to do so. In the simplest terms, it covers "manifestation," meaning if you manifest something into the world, it will likely happen. Manifesting positivity, success, and a good attitude will likely bring those things to you. On the other hand, someone who is always negative and has a poor attitude won't have the same success as someone who is manifesting success.

Resilience is also crucial. Having a positive mindset and attitude and manifesting positivity doesn't mean you don't need resilience. By resilience, I mean not caring at all if you're told no, to screw off, get hung up on, or even yelled at. It's in one ear and out the other like it never happened, and then on to the next prospect. The more you practice this, the easier it gets. You start to build thicker skin and eventually become almost numb to rejection. Instead of being sad or spooked that a prospect might call your manager, you learn to laugh about it. Rejection isn't a good thing, but it's a part of sales and life. To be successful, you need to develop thicker skin and brush off rejections like they never happened. It is important to learn from mistakes, even when faced with rejection.

Whether through e-mail or cold calls, we can always glean lessons from being told no. Why did they reject me? What could I have done better for the next call? Should I have responded to their objection differently? Should I have tailored my pitch based on their title? Should I have paused longer? The questions are endless, but the key takeaway is to always continue learning and growing. Maintaining a positive mentality and attitude also comes with practice and confidence. The more someone develops their skill set, the more confident they become. For example, a college basketball player who averages 50% from the free throw line in their freshman season likely lacks confidence and sufficient practice. If that player shoots 500 free throws a day during the offseason, by their sophomore year, their average might rise to 75%. Why? Because they practiced and gained confidence. The same principle applies to sales and any aspect of life where one seeks success.

You might wonder, if I am in sales, how can I improve my skills to build more confidence and achieve better results? Great question! There are many ways to enhance your skill set and build confidence in your daily activities and career. Thanks to technological resources, you can learn an entire skill set or sales techniques from the comfort of your home. Platforms like LinkedIn Learning, Udemy, and books, as well as following sales influencers, provide a wealth of resources. A quick Google search can offer numerous tools to enhance your skills and boost your confidence. In sales, a positive attitude and mindset are directly linked to managing stress levels. Take time to get fresh air, meditate, clear your mind, practice breathwork, snuggle with your dog, or engage in grounding exercises to reduce stress. Lowering stress levels can lead to improved mental clarity, which is beneficial in sales and other aspects of life. Take ownership of both your successes and failures. Failures are key to growth because we learn what to do and what not to do from them. By learning from your failures, you will encounter them less frequently, resulting in increased confidence, a more positive mental attitude, and better outcomes. Additionally, set goals for yourself. Achieving these goals will boost your confidence and enhance your mental well-being. Acknowledge your hard work and success when you reach a goal. Celebrate with a nice dinner or drinks, but remember you still have work in the morning!

Some people practice journaling, putting pen to paper to improve mental clarity and achieve peace of mind. This habit can help set a positive mindset for the day or wind down after a long one. Practicing gratitude by creating a daily list of things you're thankful for is another great way to maintain a positive, grateful, and happy outlook. One of my favorite lines is, "Remove yourself from the outcome and increase your income." This quote emphasizes focusing on being an expert and addressing the issue at hand rather than just making a sale. It's a powerful mindset! Mastering the art of forgetting about closing a deal and concentrating on solving problems will naturally lead to sales and income. In summary, celebrate small and big wins, learn from your failures, keep a positive mindset with daily affirmations, reduce stress, and forget about the outcome!

As an SDR, even though I exceeded my quota each month, I continued to seek feedback from both my peers and my managers. Nobody enjoys working with someone who claims to know it all. I wanted to remain grounded and ensure all co-workers knew I was open to learning new techniques and/or improving on those I already implemented. In addition to co-worker feedback, I continued to look for different online resources to help me learn, which spanned from tutorials, certifications, or even LinkedIn groups to confer with other sales professionals. In terms of mindset, knowing I wanted to be successful, I pushed myself each month to not only hit and exceed my quota, but to be ranked the top SDR each month. Although a bit of an old school mentality, I was able to quickly learn that if you want something in life, you have to go after it because nobody will just hand it to you. The same theory applies to this book – I came up with the idea of publishing a book to help sales professionals, so I created a plan and executed it. So, feel free to, literally, take a page out of my book! As I said before, although sales is not for everyone, I knew quickly that it was the right career for me because of my desire to work and learn. Because I wanted to be responsible for my own success, and because I wanted to feel fulfilled, personally, professionally, and financially, I knew a sales role would provide me with the opportunity to do so. So, as an SDR, instead of working the typical 40-hour work week, I would start early and end late, capitalizing on my ability to do more than my peers. Having said that, I challenge you to have a discussion with yourself to determine what you want to take away from your job, your career, your life, etc., and write it down. Putting it on paper, especially for me, always made it feel more real, providing you with a starting point to curate your plan before execution.

Chapter 12

MENTORSHIP, CAREER PLANS & GOALS

F inding a mentor, especially the right one for you, can significantly impact your personal and professional development and growth. You become what you surround yourself with. If you spend time with friends who don't strive for the best for themselves or you, it might be time to reconsider your inner circle. True friends will want the best for you. It can be difficult, but you'll learn who to keep close and who to let go of. Those who don't want the best for you may try to bring you down with them. With enough negativity and challenges in daily life, it's best to eliminate as much of that as possible. Transitioning from being around unmotivated people to those who are driven and successful will greatly increase your chances of success. We become what we surround ourselves with, so associate with people you consider winners if you want to be a winner. This is also why finding the right mentor is so important. Like a therapist, just because one mentor works for you doesn't mean they'll work for someone else. Find a mentor who you're comfortable with, fits your style, and can help you grow professionally and personally. Personal and professional growth are closely linked.

Choosing the right mentor can be a complex decision because you want to ensure it is the right fit for you. Remember, the mentor must also agree to the relationship. It's not as if Tony Robbins is waiting around for you to ask him to be your mentor. You'll need to put in the effort to find the right mentor. Before you start, define what you're looking for in a mentor. Most people see a mentor as someone who provides guidance, support, and knowledge. A mentor can help you navigate tricky situations more efficiently and effectively with their substantial experience. While the characteristics of a good mentor may vary, some essential qualities include experience, success, communication skills, mutual respect, compatibility, and availability. Availability is crucial; even if Tony Robbins were your mentor, his busy schedule might prevent him from being as accessible as you need.

Finding your mentor is a task in and of itself. There are many online and in-person places to search for a mentor, but where does one even begin? The first place to look is through professional networks. These can be online or in person, such as LinkedIn, professional groups, your workplace, educational institutions, online communities, and networking events. Attending these events or being an active participant can certainly help you find your mentor. For example, if you are attending a networking event over lunch for people in your industry, you might wonder how to approach the right mentor if you think you've found them.

I suggest first making an introduction and seeing if some type of commonality and rapport can be established, indicating mutual interest. If that goes well and there is chemistry, ask if they would be willing to meet. If they agree, be clear about what you are looking for, in this case, a mentor. Set specific goals, objectives, and boundaries with your new mentor to ensure mutual understanding. Once you find the right mentor, think deeply about your career goals. Your mentor can certainly help you figure this out with their years of experience. Especially if you are starting your first job or beginning your sales career, taking advice from a seasoned veteran about career goals and achieving them is a great idea. However, this is easier said than done.

I remember being a freshman in college, overwhelmed and confused about choosing my major. At 18 years old, how was I supposed to pick what I wanted to do for the rest of my life? Of course, many people change careers and goals, but if you're lucky enough to have your first choice as your only choice and stay in that field forever, kudos to you. For most of us, career changes are inevitable. If you are starting out in sales in an entry-level role, such as an SDR or BDR, you want to get your foot in the door with a company and get a job, but then what? Where do you go from there? How do you get promoted? What do you even want to get promoted to? Do you want to stay an individual contributor, focusing on selling and hitting your quota? Or do you want to aim for a management position? It's important to get an idea of the direction in which you want your career to head so you can set a clear and concise path for yourself with the help of your manager and mentor.

Your mentor and manager are great resources for helping you find the right direction. It is completely fine if you aren't sure yet, and it's also fine if your career aspirations change. Life happens, and so do changes in your plans and goals. I remember my first job as an SDR. The thought of what was next never crossed my mind when I started the role. Soon after, I thought the only next step was to get promoted to an Account Executive role. Knowing what I know now, that is not the case. I was young with no mentor and nobody to lean on, so that's what happened. If I had a mentor at the time, they could have led me down a different path that might have been more suitable for me. The point is to learn from those with more experience and wisdom. Roll with the punches, work hard in whatever you decide to do, be professional, be respectful, give it your all, find a mentor, and everything will work out!

Chapter 13

SALES ACRONYMS

SDR - Sales Development Representative (Entry Level Role)

BDR - Business Development Representative (Entry Level Role)

AE - Account Executive (Typically, an SDR or BDR gets promoted to this)

SE - Sales Executive (Typically, an SDR or BDR gets promoted to this)

AM - Account Manager

BD - Business Development

CS - Customer Success

ROI - Return on Investment

ARR - Annual Recurring Revenue

MRR - Monthly Recurring Revenue

ACV - Annual Contract Value

TCV - Total Contract Value

B2B - Business to Business

B2C - Business to Consumer

D2D - Door to Door

SaaS - Software as a Service

CRM - Customer Relationship Management

ABC - Always be closing

BANT - Budget, Authority, Need, Timeline (Style of selling)

MEDDIC - Metrics, Economic Buyer, Decision Criteria, Decision Process, Identify Pain & Champion (Style of selling)

Champion - The prospect who wants your solution and will help you throughout the sales process.

MEDDPICC - Metrics, Economic Buyer, Decision Criteria, Decision Process, Paper Process, Identify Pain, Champion, and Competition.

Disco - Known as a discovery call, the part of the meeting where the sales rep is uncovering pain points and important information.

CTA - Call to Action

ICP - Ideal Customer profile

KPI - Key performance indicators

Quota - Your personal sales goals provided by your manager/company

MQL - Marketing Qualified Lead

SQL - Sales Qualified Lead

YTD - Year-to-date

RFP - Request for proposal

SEO - Search Engine Optimization

MSA - Master Services Agreement

SOW - Statement of Work

OF - Order Form

SMB - Small to Medium Sized businesses

Enterprise - Largest Companies

GTM – Go to Market

Chapter 14
STATISTICS

Personally, I love statistics. It might come from years of following sports, but regardless, I enjoy statistics and find them useful, fun, and intriguing. So, let's take a look! The following data is sourced from Klenty, a sales engagement software company.

- The best time to make cold calls and book more meetings is between 4:00 and 5:00 PM, which is 71% more effective than calling at other times.
- On average, sales reps make 8 cold calls to the same prospect before reaching them.
- 60 cold calls a day should serve as a benchmark for reps who cold call.
- Starting a cold call with "Did I catch you at a bad time?" leads to booking 40% fewer meetings.
- Reps who give the reason for their call are more than twice as likely to book a meeting.
- The top sales reps have their "pitch" last only 12 seconds on average.

Let's have even a bit more fun with these statistics and look at some mind-blowing cold-calling statistics provided by the Brevet Group, a sales consulting and training firm.

- 92% of all customer interactions happen over the phone.
- 30-50% of sales go to the vendor that responds first.
- Thursday is the best day to prospect, followed by Wednesday.
- Nearly 1 in 8 jobs in America are full-time sales jobs (roughly 13%).
- In companies with 100-500 employees, an average of 7 people are involved in the buying process.
- A staggering 78% of sales reps who use social media outsell their peers.
- E-mail is almost 40 times more effective at acquiring new customers than Facebook and X.
- Reps who actively seek referrals tend to earn 4 to 5 times more than those who do not.
- Only 13% of customers believe a sales rep can understand their needs.
- More than half of salespeople lack the correct skills to be successful.

Leaving you with the best stat for last and my favorite: 91% of customers say they would give referrals, but only 11% of sales reps ask for them! I hope this book helps your prospecting efforts and brings you much success.

Happy hunting!

Chapter 15

CAREER GROWTH

Career growth should always be at the forefront of one's mind who is looking to build a career or increase their earnings potential. Although navigating the waters of growing one's career, or "moving up the ladder," may seem like a dauting task, it is imperative to continue your personal and professional development. This chapter, although specifically tailored to SaaS and tech sales, contains principles that can be applied across all sales fields and for use by all sales professionals.

So, how does one get into a sales position? The hardest part, speaking from personal and professional experience, is getting your foot in the door to obtain an entry level role as an SDR or BDR. Although the application process may seem daunting as most job postings require "1-3 years of sales experience," it's more likely than not that your previous role contained a sales aspect that you can rely on. However, even if you truly have zero years of sales experience, it is still worth applying for the job as most companies are looking for an individual who is personable, friendly, and most importantly, coachable. If you are able to advise the interviewer that you are coachable and open to critique, the lack of experience may be overlooked. Remember, the goal is to obtain your first role in sales to gain the invaluable experience needed to move upwards and onwards. To do so, we just need to get into the industry first!

Here's a little story of how I landed my first job as an SDR: I was 24 years old with very minimal sales experience but was yearning for a career change. Knowing myself, and knowing how motivated I was financially, I knew sales could be the right field for me. So, I drafted a resume, met with a professional to review and revise it, and I fired off hundreds of job applications via LinkedIn Jobs, BuiltIn, Glassdoor, and Indeed. My personal tip when applying for jobs on any site is to use the filters and only apply to jobs that we're posted in the past seven days or two weeks and to not apply to job postings that are thirty days old or more. As previously discussed, the theory of volume also applies to applications, which is exactly what I had done. At the end of the day, all you need is one offer and one company to believe in you enough to get your foot into the door. I applied to hundreds of job applications, I had several interviews with a number of companies, each time explaining my story and advising the interviewer of how coachable I truly was. Following the interview process, I received my first offer as an SDR, and although I wasn't thrilled about the base salary or the industry, I knew I needed to take it for the sole reason of gaining experience. Within 5 months of accepting the job as an SDR, I was promoted to

AE because of my ability to exceed quota month after month. Getting back to it. Now that you've obtained your first entry level role as an SDR or BDR, it's time to perform. Don't worry, the company knows you're new to the field and will provide support and training to ensure you're successful. For example, a "ramp up" period will likely be afforded to you to assist you in meeting your quota. On average, once you've proven successful in your role, it can take anywhere from 8 to 14 months to receive a promotion. Although beginning a new career comes with inevitable ups and downs, the materials contained within this book should certainly help you achieve your desired performance results in your new sales role.

In addition to your successful performance as an SDR or BDR, it is extremely important to relay to your manager, at the outset and during your tenure, of your career goals in becoming an individual selling contributor. Remember, if you don't ask for it or work towards it, the chances of it occurring are minimized. It's imperative to be your biggest advocate and speak up to ensure your manager is aware of your desire to grow your role, both professionally and personally. In terms of promotions, there are several different paths one can take following their tenure as an SDR or BDR. One can choose to remain in a sales-forward role as an Account Executive or, to the contrary, one can choose to join Management, Marketing, or Communications.

Whichever path you desire, be sure to advise your manager as they can provide recommendations and advice to you on building your career. If, however, you decide to proceed in a sales-forward role as an Account Executive, you may be wondering what's next. When you begin your new role, it's likely that your company will give you smaller companies and/or accounts to go after until proven successful, and then will provide you with bigger accounts, likely within the strategic or enterprise selling roles. With these roles comes longer sales cycles and more financial incentives, both salary-wise and commission-wise. In terms of scale, enterprise selling is about the highest one can go in a sales-forward role. I hope this chapter provides clarity on the subject of career path and provides insight as to how to get started in sales and achieve your end goals of promotions and financial freedom.

Professional Experience

Corey is a seasoned sales professional with extensive experience across various sales roles and industries. He has worked in SaaS (Software as a Service) sales within the media, healthcare, and pharma sectors. Additionally, Corey has experience in door-to-door sales for B2B and B2C insurance. He has held positions such as SDR, Senior SDR, Sales Executive, Account Executive, and Manager of Business Development and Lead Generation. Corey has achieved the distinction of being the best SDR in company history at two different companies: one in SaaS media and the other in SaaS healthcare. He has broken numerous records at both companies, including meetings booked, meetings delivered, qualified meetings, largest deals sourced, and revenue generated in ARR (annual recurring revenue).

Corey's notable achievements include sourcing the two biggest deals during his tenure at two different companies. One was at a media company selling to a prominent professional sports team, and the other was at a healthcare company selling to pharmaceutical and biotech firms. Corey also has extensive experience mentoring, coaching, and training SDRs, helping them succeed, grow, and get promoted to the next level in their sales careers. He has built effective sales cadences for multiple teams across various industries, yielding highly successful results and accomplishments.

Feel free to contact Corey with any questions, thoughts, comments, concerns and or feedback about his book at his personal email – cgoldman2895@gmail.com

Corey's Biography

Corey was born and raised in Long Island, New York, and now resides in South Florida. Corey is a seasoned sales professional with years of experience in different sales roles and different industries. Corey has worked in SaaS (software as a service) sales in the media, healthcare, and life sciences industries, and has experience with door-to-door sales for B2B and B2C in insurance. He has held the roles of SDR, Senior SDR, Sales Executive, Account Executive, and Manager of Business Development and Lead Gen. Corey is also very successful in working remotely from the comfort of his own home.

He has been regarded as the top SDR in company history at two different companies, exceeding his quota by 200%+ month over month, and holds the record for numbers of meetings booked, meetings delivered, qualified meetings, largest deals sources, and revenue sourced in ARR (+1,000% of ARR goal - annual recurring revenue). In addition, Corey has extensive experience in mentoring, coaching, and training SDRs, helping them achieve success, and earn promotions. As a sales professional, Corey has built effective sales cadences at each company he has worked for, each proving successful as can be gleaned from his results and accomplishments. In his spare time, he enjoys spending time with his mini golden doodles named Hank and Archie and with his family and friends. Corey is also a foodie and enjoys traveling, sports, and is a big Mets, Knicks, and Jets fan.

Reference List

1. Klenty. "Cold Calling Statistics." Klenty Blog, https://www.klenty.com/blog/cold-calling-statistics/
2. Brevet Group. "21 Mind-Blowing Sales Stats." Brevet Group Blog, https://blog.thebrevetgroup.com/21-mind-blowing-sales-stats/
3. Adobe Business. "Buyer Persona Definition." Adobe Business, https://business.adobe.com/blog/basics/buyer-persona-definition/
4. Investopedia. "Call to Action (CTA)." Investopedia, https://www.investopedia.com/terms/c/call-action-cta.asp/
5. Sprout Social. "Social Selling." Sprout Social Glossary, https://sproutsocial.com/glossary/social-selling/

www.ingramcontent.com/pod-product-compliance
Lightning Source LLC
Chambersburg PA
CBHW070348230526
45471CB00006B/2462